Notes to my

DAUGHTER

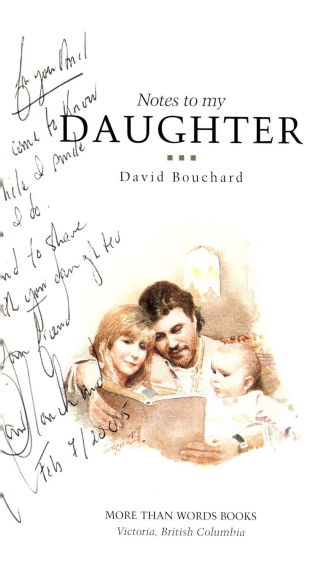

Notes to my

DAUGHTER

■ ■ ■

David Bouchard

MORE THAN WORDS BOOKS

Victoria, British Columbia

Editorial assistance by Bruce Serafin and Mark Stanton
Cover design by Ben Blackstock
Cover art by Zhong-Yang Huang
Interior art by Zhong-Yang Huang
Design by Ben Blackstock

National Library of Canada Cataloguing in Publication Data

Bouchard, Dave, 1952-
    Notes to my daughter / David Bouchard. – 1st ed.

A poem.
ISBN 1-55192-580-X

    1. Parent and child – Poetry. I. Title.

PS8553.O759N67 2002   C811'.54
C2002-902708-X
PR9199.3.B617N67 2002

1 2 3 4 5 6 7 8 9 10

Printed and bound in Hong Kong, China by
Book Art Inc., Toronto

For you, my small tomorrow,
something special that I wrote
just for you … something that
you may want to read to me
in my final moments.

■ ■ ■

CONTENTS

DEAR VICTORIA,

These pages are but a few from my journal. I've selected those that most represent the world around your mum and me as we prepared for your arrival …

Sweetheart, you were *my* idea. Your mother was not difficult to convince, but initially you were *my* dream.

Your mother and I are in the mid-years of our lives. It is no longer uncommon for couples our age to become parents, but many people do not understand why we'd choose to do so. I've often shared this journal because I find it difficult to contain my joy in you. I've found that many are interested in our experiences as we awaited your coming. I didn't think you'd mind my sharing them.

Darling, your mum and I already have four beautiful children, and yet I picture us sharing our love and our lives with you. I believe that you are the one who will never let our love die. You are the bond that will help unite our children and our families.

Sweetheart, at the time I write this letter, my dreams have all come true.

You are everything I dreamt you would be … and more. I thank God every day that you *are*. First I thank God, and then I thank your mother.

I love you so …

Daddy.

SEP
TEM
BER

■ ■ ■

September 3

We first discussed you just last week
While driving out to Sandy beach
Or English Bay or Tidley Cove
Or Stanley Park or to some mall ...

You are a thought, a simple dream
Of me and mom and of our need
To take a mammoth step in life
And go where many would not care
Nor dare to venture at our age.

You are now living in our hearts.
The ball is rolling, time is ticking,
Mother's aging and she's worried
About your feelings come sixth grade,
About you feeling that we're different,
That we're older than the parents
Of your friends and of your classmates,
That you'll somehow be embarrassed
By the fact that she's your mother.

I just smiled and rubbed the back part
Of my hand across her forehead,
Stroked my hand across her forehead,
Saying, "She'll be so much like you."

■ ■ ■

You, I know, will be as gentle,
Be as caring as *my* heaven.
You, I know, will be as kind
As she to children and to strangers.
You will never hurt a fly.
You'll be so much like your mother.
I just smiled and stroked the back part
Of my hand across her forehead.

I then talked about your eyes,
How I somehow see them looking.
And I spoke about your Roman nose —
From Granny — you'll be stately …
And the chin of your half brother
And the thick hair of your sister.
When I said that you'd have smoky eyes,
Your mom began to cry.
I then feigned a talk with you —
As though you were in the back seat.
I leaned back and talked to you -
Told you how she had been worried
That you'd somehow be ashamed,
Be embarrassed by your mother,
That you'd somehow think her less
Than you would if she were younger.

■ ■ ■

We first discussed you just last week
While driving out to Sandy beach
Or English Bay or Tidley Cove
Or Stanley Park or to some mall ...

September 11

Your mom and I are both divorced,
And soon we'll be together.
Like so many we had walked through life
Not knowing that there could be more.
No, no one ever taught me what
"From now until forever" meant.
No, no one ever taught me about
"From now until forever" ...

Made brave by love, I pondered over
What has been tradition —
Over what has been expected
From two who would give birth ...
Just how nature might allow it,
But for taboos and restrictions,
But for rules and laws unspoken
That were passed down over time.

■ ■ ■

Did not the old Gepeto want
A boy of flesh and blood —
A boy to love and one to care for —
One he'd teach and whom he'd learn from —
One he'd talk with Sunday morning
When the world seemed to have faded?
Had he not wished for a real one,
Not a boy of painted wood?

Was not his age we'd understood
To be the reason for the test?
A son he'd have if he should pass,
That if he failed, he'd live with less —
A puppet made by his own hand
To love and to caress!

And so it is that I one day
Can guide *you*, as I've found the road —
The road that leads to heaven's door —
That's led me to your mother.

"Made brave by love, I pondered…"

■ ■ ■

September 12

The reason you'll be special,
Unlike those who'll be your classmates,
Is the reason that you *are*, you see.
You *are* for more than part
Of what most think should be a family,
When two marry and have children —
You are more than what's expected
By a couple playing the part
Of a young mother and a father …
Look — the script is all around you —
You'll quickly see just what I mean —
You're much more of a star —

A star whose reason is to shine
Beyond the days when we are gone —
To share the glow, the one you'll find
When you see us together …
Me and mother — there is magic —
From deep down — we have been chosen —
You will share the glow that we have sewn
Inside your tiny heart.

■ ■ ■

September 13

I'm home again, alone with you.
My birthday party's over.
All the talk around our family
Is the new house and our wedding day.

You still remain our secret
As mom says we can't speak of you
Until we have conceived you
And you're healthy as can be.

I'm home again alone with you,
And wondering how you'll see me,
Though I know your brothers think me fine,
I've now turned forty-five
And that's an age when multiplied by two
Is closer to one hundred
Than I ever could imagine
Would be possible for me to …

■ ■ ■

Possible for me to want to
Be a father — start anew —
To share the world with one conceived
Through love and hope, and that is you —
A dream of what can come about
From all the love your mom and I
Have managed to discover in
These midyears of our lives.

September 16

The cat's out of the bag — your sister
Has become the first to know.
As mom had thought, she wants you too.
We spent the whole night naming you!

■ ■ ■

Ashleigh was ecstatic as she said
That she could hardly wait
To walk you down a busy sidewalk
Holding hands on Saturday,
Or run you by the ocean in your
Jogging stroller, just you two,
Or drive you to her girlfriend's house
(She'll have to get her license first) …
She swore to God she'd wake up
In the middle of the darkest night
To feed you and to change you …
She can hardly wait to meet you.

The secret's out — yes, Ashleigh knows
About our plan, our dream of you.

September 20

Add your brother to the list
Of those who know our little secret.
Add Etienne's name to the list
Of those who share in the excitement
That you'd hope to find in families
That are blended just as ours is —
That you'd hope to find in families
Where the parents are our age.

■ ■ ■

Etienne is quite an athlete
Yet his strength is in his caring.
Like your sister, he will be someone
Who'll watch out over you.
And he was very quick to tell us
He'd mentioned you some time ago,
And quick to tell us both how much
He wants to have you too.

We're making preparations
That we shouldn't — it's too early.
There is little we can do when asked
By those who need our trust,
Who can't help wonder what our plans are
When they see us together.
(And it's rare the moment I'm with her
That you're not with us too.)

September 28

I'm home. I just got off the phone —
Your mother calls me every night,
Just after I walk in the door,
Walk into this forsaken place.

■ ■ ■

"A few more days and nights like this
Until we are together, dear ...
A few more days and nights, you'll see,
It won't be long, my love."

I've lived my life in constant search
Of what I'd not been taught to seek,
From house to house — from town to town
For what I'd not been taught to see ...

A basement suite, a stop to sleep
To read and write, to wash and eat —
Until the world allows us both
To start our lives refreshed and new —
Until the world allows us both
To dare to dream of you.

OC
TOB
ER

■ ■ ■

October 3

Thank God you're here when I get home.
This morbid place reminds me
Of my countless cold, dark childhood days
At school out on the prairie,

The place where every night for years
I cried myself to sleep.
I was too young to be alone!
I cried myself to sleep ...

And thus the mess your mother's left
To deal with as she cares for me.
And thus the reason for my dream:
A life with her and you.

October 5

If what I've come to learn of God
Is true of you, then what you are
Is close as you will ever be
To near him as you're near to me ...

■ ■ ■

If what I've come to learn of God
Is deepest love in purest form,
Then what you are is nothing less
Than God himself, and if it's so
You're right there next to Grandpa George
(Who died when mom was only nine)
And with your uncle Adrien,
(I named your brother after him.)

Their spirits live from year to year
Through what they were and what they meant
And how they shaped your mom and me,
Through love and tender caring —
And of how they live through mom and me
And now through you, our baby.

"You are right there next to Grandpa George"

■ ■ ■

October 12
Thanksgiving Day

We're thankful, yet we worry
About the world as you might find it —
About the pressures that will come to bear
On you, our small tomorrow …
That the challenges our children face today
Will grow and fester —
That their pain and stress and worries
Will exist in your life too.

I'm sleeping at your mother's,
Not alone back in my dungeon.
I've come to say goodnight, my dream.
I know you sense my pleasure
As I know that you've been living
Since we first discussed our having you,
When mom and I dared dream aloud
While driving on that rainy day …

October 13

I've read the past few pages
That have all been penned in sunshine.
In reflecting now I'd better show
The rain you'll come to know.

■ ■ ■

I always look for brightness
In a world that's sometimes gloomy,
And I know it's not the answer:
My demons won't just melt away.

Your coming will pose hardships
For a few who won't be ready —
For the few I have not spoken of —
From a different place and time.

We both have different stories,
Me and mother, we have baggage
That at times is hard to live with
And is always somewhere near.
We have children from two others
Who are always somewhere near us,
That we love as we'll love you —
Yet, through whom we live our pasts.

We see memories at each corner
That can never be forgotten —
That remind us just how different
We were back in younger years.

■ ■ ■

This is not to sound ungrateful,
On a Sunday, on Thanksgiving,
But I've always sought out brightness
In a world that's sometimes gloomy
And I know it's not the answer:
My demons won't just melt away.

October 24

I'm sitting in my hotel
Up in Whistler. It's still early.
Most the others here are sleeping
While I sit and write to you.

It's the first time since we've dated —
Me and mother — that we've parted —
If but only for a few dark hours
We've been together night and day.

We've a lifetime to catch up on —
We need history to protect us
From the memories of events and times
Before our dream of you.

■ ■ ■

I'll seek to find the courage
And the words to share the learnings
Of a lifetime that pertains
To many things that now are clear.

I'll strive to be inspired
As I guide you toward heaven
That I've found to be right here on earth —
Not high above the clouds but here
And very much attainable
For those who learn to love and share —
Who focus on the Yin and Yang
And balance — it's the single key
To living out a healthy life:
As you take, so you should give
To others and to nature …
It's by seeking out this harmony
That you'll find God, my dear.

NOV
E M
BER

■ ■ ■

November 15

We're high above the Rockies,
Me and mother, flying United.
We're headed for New York —
The first time for either one of us.

So much has passed since last I sat
To talk to you — I've missed you!
Where to start — it's been so long —
Don't think I've stopped my wanting you.

The move is done — I'm with her now.
The house is all we'd dreamed of.
The kids are fine, the scene is set —
In fact, you might be more than words.

We'll know by Tuesday if we have
Conceived you — I can't help but smile.
You'll be the talk of all the town.
They'll talk of you all over town …

Your mom and I are noticed now.
We've been the source of gossip.
There are those who called our love
Before we knew it possible.

"The house is all we'd dreamed of."

■ ■ ■

And as for you, a norm is set
That's hard for some to swallow.
We're ready to rewrite the rules
That others might just follow.

November 20

It's done, she's tested positive,
My head is going to burst —
I can't control myself — I'm going to die
If I can't tell the world that I'm the
Luckiest — first with your mom
And now I'll have you too …
It's like a Disney show — a dream come true —
First mom and now there's you!

You're three weeks old, inside of mom.
You're growing by the minute.
You'll soon have all your fingers, toes —
Your sex has been determined.
We'll worry till we meet you
That the basics are in place.
(It's nothing more than part of life
For parents of our age.)

■ ■ ■

It's Sunday and we're headed home.
We're coming from the island.
We've been let down — we were so wrong.
The test should have been negative —
Unless we had and then lost you —
It seems to be quite common —
We're coming home — we've been deceived —
We're coming home alone …

DEC
EM
BER

■ ■ ■

December 29

It's early Monday morning.
We've been married less than two days.
We were married at St. Francis
In the Wood — I wish you'd seen it.

The vows I wrote I'll keep for you.
I gave them to our guests —
I had to hand them out on paper —
They were written as a reading
But I broke — I couldn't help but think
Of where and how we'd come from —
How we'd made it — me and mother —
I am married to your mother …

■ ■ ■

It's early, mother's sleeping.
We're in Boston and we're married.
There's just so much to tell you,
About the service, the reception,
About your brothers in tuxedos,
About your sister wearing lace.
About your mother — oh, your mother …
Where to start? You won't believe it
Without seeing it with your own eyes.
Words can only make you doubt me.
This is clearly an occasion
Where my script will need supporting
By the photos that were taken
In the rain, right in our garden …
In our home that there awaits you …
With your family that awaits you …

■ ■ ■

We've walked all throughout Boston
From the South End to the Hill,
And we're seeing all that we've dreamed of,
Rarely stopping but for one small little
Package, from the drug store,
That would tell us if you are …
Now I must not get too excited,
We were wrong when last we saw
The two red lines that mean you're fighting
To hang on to life within,
With little help but hope and prayer —
Nothing we can do but wait.
And yet, how to stop from shouting
Out my pleasure in the street —
My joy, my pride in what is happening
In that tiny, sacred place.

"I am married to your mother …"

JAN
UA
RY

■ ■ ■

January 2

It's done — another milestone —
We've spent New Year's here in Bean Town!
We stopped in every single shop,
Bought presents for the kids back home,
We ate at Joe's and dreamt about
Our future, me and mother
Of the child we know she carries.
We've tested every night to see
The X or two red lines — to read
The message sent from heaven.
(We will have to stop this practice:
Every night until your birth
Would seem extravagant — ridiculous —
I would, though, if she'd let me.)

We've started making plans
Of how we'll tell all those who matter,
How we'll take them for Chinese food,
Surprise them through a cookie —
Or we'll send them out a telegram,
A singing or a dancing one —
Or simply drop a hint or two
Through crank calls in the night!

We've planned your room — your holidays
From grade school through to college.
You're in our hearts and on our minds
Each second of our day.

January 15

Your mother is exhausted.
She is nauseous — you're the reason.
You're now six weeks and counting.
Though it's soon, she's started showing.

We've not yet told the world you are.
No — no one knows but Granny.
The kids know that we want you,
But still don't know that you exist …

We're not sure that you're healthy yet,
So no one knows but Granny …

January 24

I've seen you with my own two eyes:
Your arms, your legs (though stumps they are).
Your heart was beating wildly —
You were tucked up in the corner.

■ ■ ■

You jumped — we laughed — a new place found
You curled up in the center
Of your nest, deep in your mother ...
Of your place deep in your mother ...

We've pictures of you six weeks old.
Through sound, we've seen you small but real.
An inch or so yet clearly here -
A miracle and nothing less.

Your mother says you look like me.
(You're nothing but a stump and head.)
A miracle and nothing less ...
We now have your first picture.

FEB
RU
ARY

■ ■ ■

February 1

Your uncle Wayne has come to town —
Your mother's only brother.
He is our age and without kids,
He'd love to be the one in wait-
And so we both played down our joy
In telling him about you
Your uncle Wayne has heard it all —
That's two who know our secret ...

February 3

There's still a month or better
Till we hear if you are healthy.
There's still a month or more before
We tell the world you *are*.
And for the most part they'll be happy,
One or two won't share our pleasure —
For *their* reasons they won't want you.
For *their* reasons they won't care.

What's sad is the effect
That they'll have on a few others —
Who would love to show their pleasure
But for fear they might offend them —
Will not dare to show their pleasure,
Will not show us how they care.

February 10

Your mother's lying beside me
On the couch, where she is resting.
She is trying to recover
From a needle in her tummy —
From a test they did this morning …
We are soon to hear the news
About our baby — are you healthy?
Can we tell the world you are?

I saw you for the second time:
You're now big as a peanut.
Your hands and legs — your face being formed —
You jumped and turned — you pushed — you shoved …

Your mother's lying beside me
On the couch — she's lying here resting.
She raised her head and said:
"You know, my father called me peanut!"

■ ■ ■

February 25

It's been two weeks and no word yet
To tell us how you're doing.
Though mother's showing more each day —
Yet no one has been asking.

It won't be long before she shows
Too much to hide our secret —
You're three months old — too big to hide —
Not long our little secret …

She's feeling much less tired now.
She's hardly ever nauseous.
She's gained ten pounds since that first day —
I'll go and take her picture —
That I'll share with you, when this I read
To you, my small tomorrow —
That I'll read a hundred times or more
Each day and each tomorrow.

■ ■ ■

March 5

Your mother had a package
With my lunch — a box I knew contained
The message I'd been waiting for —
The news I longed to hear ...

Her smile said you were healthy
Though we'd guessed it by the time elapsed
Between the test she'd undergone —
Between that time and now ...
The box would tell me if my prayers
Were answered, as I told her but
Two days ago — my heart was still set
On a little girl -

Within I found a tiny suit
A top, some pants, three pairs of socks —
All these were knit in softest pink:
Your top and pants — *in softest pink!*

March 24

The world now knows that you exist.
We told the kids, who did the rest.
The playground was all talking
By the time we picked up Ashleigh ...

■ ■ ■

In a world as small as ours is,
Word can travel fast as sound —
So there's not a soul who doesn't know,
The weight is less, now that they know.

Reaction, as we guessed, was mixed.
Elation from our closest friends,
Our family was delighted,
But for one you'll come to know.

(Today we lost our Amber
Whose eleven years with mother
Mean a dark cloud in our home awhile.
I wish you'd seen her old dog smile.)

APRIL

■ ■ ■

April 25

I don't know where to start …
It's been so long since last I wrote to you …
We've bought your bed — it's lovely
Like a wooden sleigh — mahogany —
And a chair to match your bassinet —
Your linen is of ivory …

We've built a little house for you,
Exactly like our own to scale,
With window boxes — a Dutch door —
A roof with tiny shingles.

You'll have your own small garden —
Sit back on your deck and watch us —
When we tire you'll invite us
Up for tea — in your small garden.

M
A Y

■ ■ ■

May 4

You've now become real strong
With all your pushing and your kicking.
Your mother's put on so much weight —
I dare not write the number down —

We read aloud to you each night.
Your favorite book is *Junie B.*
It's sitting in your nursery ...
We are nesting in your nursery ...

May 8

It's now two days from Mother's day.
She just turned forty-three.
I signed a sweet card with your name —
It said I knew what kind of girl you'd be:
A caring and a thoughtful one —
You'll be in every way like her.
We had a lovely feeder built:
From you, with love, to mother ...

She's lying in bed right next to me.
It's early in the morning
When I write to you most often —
Dark and early in the morning.

"We are nesting in your nursery."

■ ■ ■

Mother's Day

If ever there's a time
That we should celebrate a Mother's day,
It should be as we live through
All these changes day to day ...
At first she felt unwell — that passed —
Her back has ached for six months straight.
Her body's stretched. She's put on so much weight.
Small veins show on her legs.
She's trouble sleeping, can't stop eating,
Yet she smiled at me and said:
"You know, I've never been as happy
As I am this mothers day ..."

May 18

Today she pinched a nerve.
It struck her half way down the stairs.
She cried and froze — she dared not move.
I helped her knowing that she'd worked too hard.

We smiled and laughed and wondered
If you somehow felt that pain,
And if you feel the joy you bring
To me and mother with each passing day.

"From you, with love, to mother …"

JUNE

■ ■ ■

June 9

The task with which I'm charging you,
My loving small tomorrow
Is to never let the magic die
Between me and your mother.

You'll come to see how most are born
As part of what's expected —
Just how few there are whose lives begin
For reasons quite as gentle.

Thus I see you as a messenger,
Also sent from heaven,
One who's quest is somewhat much like his —
That started with *his* mother.

June 19

Your mother's forty three,
Considered older by most standards —
Thus we're looking at the options
For your birth — our minds are open.
Two long labors and the memories
Over time not even dampened —
Things have changed so much it's likely
A cesarean that will happen ...

■ ■ ■

I can't help think you'll find this
Much more pleasant way of meeting her —
Though through it, I will be the one
Who sees and holds you first.

There's a holding room to keep
Your family waiting — they'll be anxious
Just as we are for your coming —
Less than six weeks — you are coming —
Just the thought of you — I smile and cringe —
I can't wait till we meet.

JULY

■ ■ ■

July 4

You're now three pounds and very strong —
We watch you morn and evening.
We love it when you move about —
We push you and we probe you.

Our thoughts are on your health,
The smile we know you have by now —
The shape and colour of your eyes ...
The form and texture of your face.

(I'll see you and I'll hold you first —
And turn to where she lies in wait
And through a special smile
I'll tell her if you have *her* eyes.)

July 31

It's three weeks now and counting —
Mother's huge — we've not seen bigger
But for two who carried twins.
We smile each time we see a head turn —

■ ■ ■

She's not slept through the night
For several weeks — she's up and down.
Her ankles swell unless her feet are up.
She's numb on her right side.
The doctor said she's doing just fine.
She lost some weight this week.
She is the picture of good health.
She'd love to stay this way forever.

AUGUST

■ ■ ■

August 8

She's bursting at the seams, your mother's
Massive — we've but two weeks now.
The doctors say you're healthy,
Strong and active — only two weeks now.

We've nested — we are ready —
You can join us any moment now —
There aren't two parents anywhere
Who want their baby more than we.

August 10

They've moved your birthday up a week.
We've now but days to wait —
We're just like kids on Xmas Eve —
Our angst — our hearts are going to burst!

We're as ready as we'll ever be
It seems that you are too —
We've now but days before we meet
Our tiny girl — our dream come true!

"Only two weeks now …"

■ ■ ■

Your mother's speaking from our bed
(It's Monday of the week you come):
"I'm thinking of how hungry
That I know I'll be on Friday ..."

We now have only five days left
Until your sacred voyage
For us the meeting of the path
We know will lead to heaven.

August 14

It's early in the morning —
Four Eleven — it is dark.
Your mother's tossing and she's turning —
I can't sleep 'cause it's your birthday ...
It's early Friday morning —
The fourteenth — this blessed day —
The day we hoped would take forever —
That we wished would take forever ...

We know how blessed we are —
We've loved each second of your coming
In a way that we just couldn't
In our youth — before we'd lived ...

■ ■ ■

And we know how blessed we were
To find each other when it seemed …
Just when it seemed the door to love was shut
And then came you *for love* —
Not merely for a family new …
To start a brand new life with you …

It's early in the morning —
Four eighteen — we both are anxious —
I'm soon to meet you face to face —
I'm soon to see your eyes.

… It's almost five — I'd best lie down
And hold you both together —
Let me not forget how good it feels
To hold you tight — together.

August 15

You're one day old. Where to begin?
You'd best go get the pictures.
Mom was awfully brave, as you were dear,
Just like in all the pictures …
A spinal block, a cut, a voice
Describing a big head — we looked —
Your cry next sparked your mom to tears —
They weighed you — get the pictures.

■ ■ ■

It's done. The thing is over.
It took minutes from the start to end.
The team of doctors commented
On what they saw as being so large:
Your head and hands — a perfect child
Without a flaw — *a perfect child!*
It's done — the thing is over —
You're our fairy tale come true ...

I gave you your first bath and meal —
I changed you ten times over.
You ate *very* well, you burped and slept —
A model little lady.
You had friends and gifts the whole day long —
You're round and dark and pretty.
You're everything we'd dreamed you'd be,
Our darling little baby ...

But the reason you are special
Unlike those who'll be your classmates —
Is the reason you're alive, you see:

■ ■ ■

You are far more than part of what most
Think should be a family,
When two marry and have children —
You are more than what's expected
By a couple playing the part
Of a young mother and a father …
Look — the script is all around you —
You'll quickly see just what I mean
You're much more of a star —

A star whose reason is to shine
Beyond the days when we are gone —
To share the glow, the one you'll find
When you see us together …
Me and mother — there is magic —
From deep down — you have been chosen
To share the glow that we have sewn
Inside your tiny heart.

ABOUT THE AUTHOR

David Bouchard is a popular speaker and writer. He speaks to educators, parents and students about his passions: books and reading. Some of his best-selling books include: *If You're Not From the Prairie, The Elders are Watching, The Great Race, The Mermaid's Muse, The Dragon New Year, Buddha in the Garden* and *Qu'Appelle*. David, Vicki and their daughter Victoria live in Victoria, British Columbia.